Drinking Guinness With the Dead

(Poems 2007-2021)

Justin Hamm

Spartan Press

Spartan Press
Kansas City, MO
spartanpress.com

Copyright © Justin Hamm, 2022
First Edition: 1 3 5 7 9 10 8 6 4 2
ISBN: 978-1-952411-85-4
LCCN: 2021950622

Cover photo: Justin Hamm
Author photo: Justin Hamm
All rights reserved. No part of this publication may be reproduced or transmitted in any form or by any means, electronic or mechanical, including photocopying, recording or by info retrieval system, without prior written permission from the author.

Acknowledgments

Some of these poems have appeared in the following publications, for which grateful acknowledgement is made.

I-70 Review, January Review, San Pedro River Review, MAYDAY Magazine, Sugar House Review, River Styx, Escape into Life, The Mexico Ledger, Euphony, Light: A Journal of Poetry and Photography, The Tower Journal, Stoneboat, Ghost City Review, New Reader Magazine, Up North Lit, Midwestern Gothic, Glass: A Journal of Poetry, Modern Poetry Quarterly Review, Pittsburgh Poetry Review, Common Ground Review, Lascaux Review, New Plains Review, Rust + Moth, The Good Men Project, Atticus Review, apt—a literary magazine, The Midwest , Quarterly, Storm Cellar, Hobble Creek Review, Digital Americana, Heron Tree, Oxford Magazine, Pale Horse Review, Quiddity, Big Muddy, Punchnel's, The Country Dog Review, Cedars, Referential Magazine, Hiram Poetry Review, Rougarou, Foundling Review, Emprise Review, Cold Mountain Review, Nimrod, Willow Review, The Chaffey Review, and *decomP*

Table of Contents

Foreward by Justin Hamm
Foreward by Michael Meyerhofer

Drinking Guinness with the Dead

Gratitude for the Poets / 1
Photograph / 3
Waltzing Toward Hospice / 4
Drinking Guinness With the Dead
   During a Pandemic / 5
Ghost Calling / 6
Subdivision, Small Town Missouri,
   Fifth Day of Protests / 8
Creation Story / 9
First Flight: Chicago to Keflavik / 12
Snaefellsness Peninsula / 13
In Iceland one afternoon I touched a horse / 14
Insulin Dependence Blues / 14
Quartet / 16
a young guy he asked me he said / 17
Animal Behavior / 18
Hermiting / 19
Fable / 20
Shower Beer / 24
Marriage (Detail #2) / 26
The smallest crowd ever to attend one
   of my readings / 27
The Reason / 28

The Inheritance

Don't want much— / 31

I Will Tell You Where I've Been / 32

Ohio County, Kentucky, 1985 / 34

The Carpenter / 38

Sometimes, in the good old films, / 40

Stranger at the Only Filling Station
   in Kingston, Arkansas / 41

Three Stanzas Ending With God / 43

Pilgrim / 45

Tribute / 47

Sleeping in the Town of My Birth / 48

Panic Attack / 50

After the Argument / 52

Pelicans / 55

A Moment in Kansas / 56

The Inheritance / 57

Hovland, Minnesota / 62

The most we can hope for / 64

Storm, Rural Missouri / 66

Colorado / 67

American Ephemeral

Federico Garcia Lorca Blues / 68

Worried Playground Daddy's Blues / 71

Oklahoma / 73

Begin with a whole boy, / 74

In Little League once / 76

First Lesson in Meat, 1984 / 78

If Only Ken Burns / 80

Barn Jamboree, Rosine, Kentucky / 81

First Lesson in Ephemerality / 84

The Farmers at Their Morning Coffee / 87

Arthur and Marie, 1961 / 89

Farmer, Clutching Chest / 91

Old Men Laughing on a Park Bench
   in Early October / 92

First Lesson in Vietnam, 1987 / 93

I Take Forty-Five Minutes to Shoot a Portrait
   of My Father / 94

Playing Blues Harp Alone in an
   Unfinished Basement / 96

Late August / 99

Marriage (Detail) / 101

Children in the Middle Ages / 102

Museum Guard's Blues / 103

Three days driving through scrubby desert
   and semi-arid mountain, / 105

First Lesson in the Dead / 107

Payphones in the Underworld / 108

Lessons in Ruin

From the Poet / 113

The Boy From Stanford, Illinois, (population 670)
   Sees the Van Gogh / 115

Bird on a Wire, 1989 / 116

Hooky Bobbers, 1992 / 118

Sunrise Subterfuge (in the first person) / 120

The Best Friend's Lament / 123

At Sixteen / 125

That Morning As We Slept in Our
   First House Together / 127

Goodbye, Sancho Panza / 129

The Flour Epiphany / 131

Illinois Route 3 / 133

One More Moon / 135

To Charlie / 137

Elegy for Sounds Forgotten / 139

Afterpoem / 140

Just Before Sleep / 141

In Case You Were Wondering / 142

Acclimation / 143

The Everyday Parade / 145

First Lesson in Ruin / 147

Poem For Saturday / 149

The Last Year on the Farm / 151

To a Folksinger Just Arrived From the Midwest / 152

Last Lesson in Ruin / 153

Rustsong / 154

Rebekah Just When the Drought Was Ending / 155

The Sting of the Jellyfish / 157

The Third Day of Winter / 159

God / 160

A Real Team Effort / 162

2020. Good Lord. I did what I imagine most of us did all year: rubbed my eyes early each morning, then spent the rest of the day blinking them in disbelief at the strange and unsettling state of the world. I worried. I ate too much. I lived for long periods in the alternate universe of Zoom. I drank Guinness. I tried to figure out third grade math. Prayed for the sick and dying. Lectured my old man over the phone about safety precautions. Wondered if I was doing enough to protect others from sickness myself. Felt guilty about not writing a novel or two, learning a new language, or jogging my way into the best shape of my life.

Sometimes, late at night, the Guinness might tell me to look back through old family photos. To write to friends I missed. To stream episodes of M*A*S*H* or highlights from 80s baseball games. And, eventually, to reread my first three books of poetry. First, I took some of the poems I felt most comfortable reading aloud and made a spoken word/music EP with my friend Dave. Then, one stouty night, feeling a little blue and lonely, while reading especially some of the forgotten poems I hadn't read to myself or an audience since they were published, I had the idea to represent the last thirteen or fourteen years of writing in a single book, to give those poems I'd cast aside another chance. I didn't imagine there would be a path to allow that to happen, and I can't express how grateful I am that Jason Ryberg at Spartan Press has given me a chance to collect my work that way.

It's good to have so many of my poems under one cover to share with folks who have never read my work before. And for those who know my poems from earlier books, thank you. I hope you gain a richer perspective on them from *Drinking Guinness with the Dead*.

-JH

As I write this, I just so happen to be strapped into a chair several thousand feet in the air, passing slowly over a Midwestern checkerboard of straight-edged fields and broad, irregular lakes. I mention this because the world is filled with so many stunning things that it's easy to become desensitized. Sometimes, we need a reminder—the kind that flips tables and screeches across the senses like a big screen theater. Other times, though, flickers of quiet amazement slip into our lives like sunset through the window blinds or the chords of a Bob Dylan song playing in the next room.

I've been following Justin Hamm's poetry ever since *The Everyday Parade / Alone With Turntable, Old Records*, a uniquely cool chapbook where the second half is read by flipping it like a record (or a tape in an old 80s boom box). In addition to that chapbook's creative use of form, the poems themselves resonate with an uncanny blend of raw nostalgia and lyrical refinement—not to mention a hard undercurrent, a kind of cynical hopefulness, like rolling hills with thick veins of iron snaking through.

Often, a poets' first collection is their best. That's not really a surprise; the first book has a lot to overcome and a long time to simmer. But here's the thing about Justin: somehow, every collection is his best. That is, each of his artistic works—from poems to photographs—finds a new way to stand out without sacrificing that vital sense of artistic honesty... because that's what happens when brilliance gets inoculated against pretension. Because while effort and revision count for a lot, you know if you really want to create something worth its salt, you need to make honesty and personal investment your religion. And here's a poet who already knows that lesson down in his bones, the same way farmers know the value of a solid wheel and a sharp blade.

Justin's latest collection begins with gratitude for the *blood of peaches* and all those poets who have taken the time *to polish the face of the moon* and *bottle the acid of all / the wars I never had to fight.* That word, gratitude, sums up Justin perfectly. Not long ago, I was chatting with him in the hallway after one of his readings and a young audience member shyly approached to let him know how much his words meant. I've seen faux humility before—we all have—but there's no faking what fills the eyes when someone you don't even know takes the time to thank you for something you've made (especially when you made it for precisely the right reasons).

There's a lot more to be said about Justin's poetry—including the fact that one of his pieces, *Goodbye, Sancho Panza,* has been studied by literally tens of thousands of students worldwide—but maybe what amazes me the most is Justin's respect for the world his poems inhabit. His quiet insistence that, appearances to the contrary, you and I are worth writing about—and because this is Justin Hamm we're talking about, you know it'll be done right.

-Michael Meyerhofer, *What To Do If You're Buried Alive*

For Mel

*I just like a good, sad song.
The sadder, the better.
It moves me.*

-John Prine

Gratitude for the Poets

Thank you for the blood of peaches
and the scarecrows boogying in the breeze.

Thank you for taking the time
to polish the face of the moon.

Thank you for your slant rhymes
and your lovely lyric wind chimes.

Thank you for the beers, the coffee,
the warm cookies. Especially the beers.

Thank you, poets, for your postcards
from the inner circles of hell

and for speaking your particular spells
into the shade of death.

Thank you for Wednesday night church
and all fifty-two ways light can fall upon a leaf.

Thank you for the broken pencil tips.
Thank you for teaching me butterflies

have hearts inside their wings.
Thank you for sneakers on city pavement

and for bottling the acid of all
the wars I never had to fight.

Thank you for the mangers in your lips
and the tears in your guitars.

Thank you for knowing. And wondering.
Doubting, suggesting, insisting.

Thank you for your loyal horses
and your dark woods filling with snow.

For your pool sharks shirking school
and the judgment of the midday sun.

For the invisible drums thrumming
beneath your pyrotechnical songs.

For the ten-minute vacations
and the laying on of hands.

Thank you, poets, for giving
love its own language.

Thank you for giving language.
Thank you for giving love.

Photograph

My grandfather in
red suspenders

and white t-shirt,
dyed-dark hair loose,

favorite feed cap
held against his hip.

He stands beside
a fledgling juniper

that will someday
shade his grave.

Ten-thousand days
ago this was.

You could still find
peach soda in Ohio County.

Dali had it wrong.
The years melt.

The clocks continue,
brutal as prison guards.

Waltzing Toward Hospice

In the brief silence between summer storms
"The Missouri Waltz" sobs from the speakers
of a slow-idling van.

A muscled man in white wheels an old woman
down a long, floral-carpeted hallway.

Near the front door a pile of her late husband's
carpentry sketches rots atop the rough cushion
of a faded armchair.

Spools of unused thread lay tipped over and scattered
like tiny sarsen stones on an end table.

Outside in the godawful Ozark humidity a boy on a
bike slows so a girl in a backwards ballcap
can catch up to him.

Drinking Guinness With the Dead During a Pandemic

They arrive, quite uninvited, set up in their invisible folding chairs, tilt their unseen containers, and cross their weightless legs. They do not speak. You have already been drinking. Drinking and debating whether regret is a tiny, panicked bird thrashing in a cage or a comet burning toward a future intersection. The dead, as a rule, divulge no part of what they might have gathered from the other side. You do not ask them. You have just entered week eight of isolation. You know too much of late-stage claustrophobia to spoil their brief escape. They must return soon to cluttered attics, cobwebbed rafters of barn-red barns, or the drum-empty caverns of purgatory. So you sit. Sip in silence. Watch your two daughters pass back and forth like little actresses across the wide screen, the wind off the back field turning their hair to galloping horses. Your mother once told you she always knew you were not born for your own times, as if there had been some mixup between the assembly line and the timekeepers. In light of that, everything makes an approximate sort of sense. Anyway, the beer tonight is especially good. The world . . . remains the world. You are in it, for now. You get the feeling the dead appreciate your silence. After all, who are you to demand to know if the eye of God is anything more than the shape of an open flower?

Ghost Calling

What I can say for certain
is some days our ghosts
just won't visit.

And some days
the Illinois landscape
becomes a ghost,
frozen fog clinging
to corn stubble
and winter weed
in the field out back
where I take the
black pup to romp.

The cycle of throw and grab,
of flee and return,
until even the pup
grows bored and gallops off
to sniff around
at frost-marbled ground.

Isn't this just how our ghosts
must feel? Surely they tire
of returning again and again
to the same old songs
of grief, regret, apology?

I understand that now.
Next time you return
I will pour some red wine.
I will keep my sad words
in a pocket with a button.
We can finally move the table
and dance as you could
never convince me in life.

If you can hear me, wife,
I have left the lamplight
in the front room glowing.

Subdivision, Small Town Missouri, Fifth Day of Protests

All quiet, except for the growl
of a lawnmower, a child
squealing now and then.
Chirping birds gathered
around backyard feeders.
The smell of butchered cow
burning on a charcoal grill.
A father and son walk
their guns, careful to obey
all the pertinent leash laws.
They carry plastic bags
to clean up any casings
dropped on neighbor's lawns.
An officer cruises through
on his daily safety patrol,
waving a free hand to power-
walking women pumping
their May-pale arms in unison.
In house after house the news
goes on and right back off.
The sunlight on the pavement
a bright white, so white
it is almost blinding.

Creation Story

This story begins
with a father-thing,

a once-mighty
and now-gnarled relic,

scriptures in motor oil
and faded green ink

lining the sundark
papyrus of his chest.

He spits rotten teeth
and pisses pure blood

so every last note
his sons ever pick

will sound just like
real bone

scraping against
real bone.

He uses a belt
to make his points,

swollen knuckles
for punctuation.

Love? A luxury,
like a glass for beer

or a bandage over
an open wound.

Yet later, when none
remain to dispute it

some soul will decide
to rename all this love.

Will turn torches of tongue
into tough wisdoms,

the sickening smack
of rage on flesh

into hard-but-essential
education against

the dark intentions
of modern pussification.

They will say it,
will believe it

even after lips sip
from uncapped bottles

and bodies wake in
strange ditches

and fingers feel for
and find the triggers.

First Flight: Chicago to Keflavik

At 30,000 feet I photograph the sunset.
Fall asleep and dream of the time
my old man dropped five feet from a ladder

and bounced off the winter-cold concrete
outside our trailer, eyes rolling and white,
low gurgle of panic humming in his throat.

When I wake an hour later to a new sun,
I realize the hum is only the groaning
of the airplane's engine. Through the clouds

I glimpse pockets of glass-blue sea
six miles down and consider how cold
it must be among the whales and porpoises.

I press closer to you, find that place on your neck,
the scent by which I'd know you if my eyes
turned to ash or my ears sealed with rubble.

Before we left, you spoke of a will; I avoided it.
Now, the first song on my playlist shuffle, Jeff Bridges:
Funny how fallin' feels like flyin'—for a little while.

I pull my earbuds out, surrender to the engine.
Try to decide if 30,000 feet is high enough
to actually make out the old gods' laughter.

Snæfellsness Peninsula

Even the name is uneven, tumbling
off of unaccustomed tongues.
Sheep hunkered under hillside rocks.
Beautiful, squat, Beatle-maned horses.
Lava fields brightly-mossed to the horizon
and fishing villages, bluffside, guarding
beaches the color of absolute night.
In the distance, Snæfellsjökull, both
volcano and glacier, like a cold star
rising toward the slurred light of the auroras.
I remember the tiny coffee cups.
Interlacing our frozen fingers.
Puzzling over Kjarval the painter
and squinting the ancient sagas to life.
The way the air everywhere smelled
but only faintly of sulphur.
And finally, how the old grudges melted
as we saw the pure absurdity of anger
in a place where the very earth
beneath our feet constantly
rumbles with uncertainty.

In Iceland one afternoon I touched a horse

a lovely, smooth, blonde-maned horse
friendly, muscular, half-wild
and my heart/soul did not heal
not exactly
but I was pleased to find myself
in something of a James Wright poem
thinking to hell
with performance evaluations
weed whackers and research
on variable interest rates
straight to hell with pistol-cocked
egos and moral puritans
thinking as I petted his velvet forehead
and stroked his tan muzzle
and he pressed into my armpit
that for a minute it was good
to have no cell phone service
to stand and touch and breathe
to watch the sharp peaks pierce
hazy clouds in the distance
to have immediate quarrel
with neither humankind nor wind
to whisper soft and adoring
and foolish American nonsense
into the ear of this proud horse -
this lovely, smooth, blonde-maned horse
this muscular, friendly, half-wild horse
I was fortunate enough to touch
one afternoon in Iceland

Insulin-Dependence Blues

What grows exhausting
is all the unseen mindwork,
the necessary fidelity
to such precise routine,
the *faith* required
after ten-thousand tiny
sharp finger pricks
and a couple thousand more
quick hot belly jabs.

This is good for me.
This is helping me.
I will not die young.
I will

> *not*
> *die*
> *young.*

It's like trying to love
the pot-holed road
for being, at least,
some sort of a road.
Or looking up at the stars
over Lake Michigan
in hypothermic December
and trying to believe,
though we feel no heat,
every one of them
is a mighty ball of fire.

Quartet

Down by the riverside
the sad ringing of old men
on homemade guitars.

Two men play.
One man sings.

*Baby, all this foul news
that rots inside me—
I know it can wait.
It was already 'bout
ten-thousand years old
when I was born . . .*

The singer trails off;
he's forgotten
the words again.

The fourth man reaches up
and turns the brittle
pages of the moon.

a young guy he asked me he said

well what about a father's loneliness?
i said a father's loneliness
hesitates at the door
behind which dancing daughters
sing jewels into their eyes

i said it's the time-long breeze
through the yawning window
that causes the toddler's artwork
to shiver on the walls

it's shadows over a sandbox
shoes with anxiety soles
it's a radio dial a dark

and delicate gymnasium
spinning years for windows
where the prize of silence
turns out to be something more
like a collision of opposing songs

Animal Behavior

I must've been just seven or eight
when I first saw an idiot squirrel
cross unharmed over four wide lanes
only to veer back into the terrible
death rush of evening traffic.

There was a sickness of the stomach
that only worsened as the years revealed
how we men and women are like this too.

How we fight our way free, only for
the old Trouble to grin and wink again
over top the forks and plates, napkins and tables
in the tiny roadside cafe we thought safe.

The bastard nods his head toward the exit,
and just like that we rise from our stools,
drop our twenties, forgetting the apple pie,
shoulders already turning from salvation.

Hermiting

Here in the woods whole weeks pass
when the dead feel closer than the living.
The fox visits the big window each morning.
The trees call out in romance languages
while the fish stay mostly to themselves.
Yet there is far less peace than he imagined.
The old tattoo grows heavy on his arm
and changes like accelerated seasons.
Anchor. Royalty. Fire. Dove.
It's too late now for codes in the thunder.
After all, the rope on the shelf has collected
so much dust one would have to know
precisely where to look in order to use it.

1.   Fable

There were two dogs
loping along a dirt road
somewhere in Georgia.
The first was named Southern Comfort.
The other had a head cold
and carried a letter
from the American Revolution.
When the blackbird descended
on her iron-tipped wings,
the language of warranty
bleeding from her beak,
both dogs lay down and played dead
in the cabbie's rearview mirror.

2.   Abel

God is on
the side
of the martyrs,

supposedly.

3.   Fable

Segovia backs Garcia Lorca
at a flamenco festival in Spain.
This is in 1922.
On the road to Granada
before the event
Lorca encounters two dogs
who seem to be dead.
He composes a poem on
the spot to mourn them.
Once he is out of earshot
the dogs rise up, laughing.
When Lorca arrives before
the great walls of the Alhambra
he finds himself unable
to stop sneezing.

4.   Unable

A patriot soldier crouches
beside a dying flower.
Reaches out to touch
the straining stem
and the wilting petals.
The bird in his head whispers
that he should flee,
but his legs must disagree

with the dark magic
of common horse sense.
Behind him someone
with authority waves
forward toward slaughter,
making the shape of vicious
words with his mouth.

5.   Fable

A blackbird is a bullet
the way a bullet is a blackbird,
the man with no fingers
tells his son as he strokes
the two dogs at his side.

But words don't mean
anything to the boy,
who is already imagining
the dark alley through which
his brother moves on his way
home from the arcade.

6.   The End

Which is all just to say: imagine
a battle so successful

the only things left moving
are a single oil-black feather
twisting and gleaming
like a fish loose in the wind
and two dogs reciting a poem
about the senseless casualties
of the Spanish Civil War.

Shower Beer

You have heard perhaps
of this small grace

after a long day
of grueling labor

or of dealing, say,
in retail

with the shabby
American public.

Visiting your mother
in assisted living,

your nephew
on the cancer ward.

Scrubbing shit stains
from public toilets.

Shingling a roof.
Raising up a child

or an emotionally
stunted lover.

Striving to meet your
pillow with integrity.

It ought to be
glacially cold.

It ought to come
in a colorful can.

Press to each temple
for a ten count

then crack open
and slowly sip

beneath the rain
like gentle flames

crawling across
the flesh map

of tectonic tension
we call neck

and shoulders
and back.

Discard can.
As necessary, repeat.

Marriage (Detail #2)

You have been fighting. At the restaurant, to taunt her,
 you lean over
and whisper, "I'm just going to kill you with kindness."

She rips into her lemon chicken, pauses, says, "That's good
 to know—
I'm going to kill you with a knife."

Then, that long moment of silence as you wait and wait
and finally realize she really isn't going to laugh.

The smallest crowd ever to attend one of my readings

was a lone grandmother in futuristic spectacles
who I worried had wandered in by mistake.
But she was a keen listener who sighed and placed
her hand to her chest at all the right moments.

God bless her.

In fact she was only a hair less enraptured
than the folks at this birthday party I once attended
where an admittedly gifted clown sat on a stool,
blinking his makeup-caked eyes and twisting
balloons into strange shapes from every kingdom,
phylum, genus, and species ever to feature
in a special on the Discovery Channel.

He was quite good. Even the adults were hopeless
with admiration, lifting their souvenirs to the light,
whistling, grinning and shaking their heads.
"He's an *Artist*," somebody's dad or uncle proclaimed,
and a murmur of agreement circled the room.
On a nearby table a coffee can overflowed with tips.

I'm not really bitter. I have always believed
jealousy can be a fine teacher, if we allow it.
From my distant corner, I nudged the cat away
with the toe of my shoe. Wiped the green
frosting from my mustache and began to write
everything down in my pocket notebook
under the heading "ideas for future readings."

The Reason

In Arkansas once,
near the Buffalo River—
I wonder if you remember.
The loneliest bull elk
left in America slowly
lifted his racked head
and looked around
a vast, empty field.
It was nearly dark,
the first faint stars
blinking to life above.
A rare moment of quiet
in our car. Even the girls
seemed enchanted.
Me—I saw myself precisely
as I would be if I ever
lost you or those babies.
Uncertainty of movement.
Afloat in a field of nothing.
Almost too much effort
even to lift my thorny head.
Which is all just to say
I love you more than
these meager words convey.
And this is the reason
I have brought you
an enormous crate of tacos.

From *The Inheritance*

Don't want much—

just to write one little poem, sharp
as obsidian, to snake-charm time
and preacher-heal cynicism,
to build a ladder to the distant stars
and live two-thousand eighty-six years
in the hearts of Danish schoolchildren
deep in the belly of the immortal raven.

I Will Tell You Where I've Been

Look off in the direction
the weathervane points,
past the place where rain
raps sideways against the silo,
a stranger touching
the shoulder of a stranger
before asking permission to pass.

Look beyond the chrome plant.
It gleams like a future metropolis,
crying out corn steam
white as the teeth
of the pastor's eldest son.

There, where warped-wood trestles
teeter over wildflower prairie
seasoned with primrose, goatsbeard,
sneezeweed and bristly buttercup—
that is the place I have been.

I went to walk along the banks
of the muddy creek, though I should
have known better. My heart is still
my heart, and I have not prayed
in earnest since I was a child.

Would you believe me if I swore
I only go there after a downpour?
That is when you can hear her rushing,
bubbling up. Sobbing, like my mother,
for all the children she's swallowed
in the holy name of love.

Ohio County, Kentucky, 1985

1.

I stand in our
ancestor's field
all of Kentucky
a green inferno
at my back

I stand there in
one shoe
Grandmother trying
goddamnit
to get ahold of me
so as to spit shine
my filthy face

Grandfather picks through
the warped-wood barn
for his history
before the coal company
has its way

The air in this place
is ripe
with some kind
of weather

2.

They called my grandfather's
grandfather The Preacher
and that is what
he was

This land was his land

He rode these backhills
in his black coat
carrying the hidden ear
of judgement
close to his heart

His whip they say
he kept down inside
his saddlebag

I see him that afternoon
me as I told you
in his field
in my one shoe
don't ask me how

and when
the corpse of him
opens its vast red mouth
the crows pour out
like the shadows
of a thousand diamonds

3.

All around us
the insects whine

All around us
Kentucky like one
great green blaze
of summer

Grandmother closes in
reaches for the sleeve
of my t-shirt

I see the dead man
out there on his mount

I hear him speak
the bodies of those
dark birds

I know the family
secrets

I know all of them

The skies now
the color of healing
bruises

I look up
into Grandmother's
horse-wild eyes

I let her catch me

The Carpenter

Sawdust drifted
against his bootsoles

Fingers calloused,
palms ghosted white
by drywall mud

Who knows vibration
of circular saw
and router

Who knows
the hieroglyphs
of practical geometry

Whose pencil pins
stray hairs
behind his ear

Who also grasps
the cold algorithms
of construction

The utter violence
in his tools

The slicing
and the striking

The ripping
and the binding

All necessary
to build or repair

This knowledge
too
lives quietly
in his hands

Sometimes, in the good old films,

wrenches turn
and on roll
the eighteen wheelers.
And people
still make love
to their cigarettes.

This poem is for
the men whose fathers'
tool belts have been taken.

They stare
from tattered recliners
through beer-blurred eyes
down cinematic highways
that seem
to stretch on forever,
much like unemployment.
Eventually they begin
to wonder whether
sun-baked asphalt
might make
a decent bed.

This poem is for
those men.
And it comes with
a can of Coors

Stranger at the Only Fueling Station in Kingston, Arkansas

He's a songwriter, he tells us.
Used to sleep in Nashville, Tennessee.
Now he keeps a ranch up over
that middle mountain.

Says he wrote quite a few
of John Denver's early songs
under a different man's name,
which I know isn't true,
but there is no doubting
the whiskey barrels of grief
behind his wide, yellow eyes.

My wife is passed six months, he tells us.
When the nine angels come
to claim my bones too
I traded them my front two teeth
for a little more time
to make up words in the dark.

Cigarette smoke leaks
from that very toothgap
as he laughs his bullfrog laugh
and makes a guitar gesture
down around his hips.
Then his face slackens, lips
beginning to lightly tremble.

They come from the mountain, he says.
Their faces cold as the moon's.
I wasn't ready for them, he says.
Jesus, he says, I was still sweeping
her hair from the corners of our room.

Three Stanzas Ending With God

1.

Through a ragged church's
single-window eye,
miles of narrow hallway
strangled in weed and vine.
Here you could pursue
a whisper for centuries
backward or forward—
either leads directly
to the cold lips of God.

2.

The adjacent field:
two barns teeter and tilt
away from one another
like jealous siblings
trapped too long inside
the same car or family.
If the first ever decides
to shove the second over,
this is but one more way
we might make measure
of the swirling moods of God.

3.

The heron leaps off the page
of the Chinese poem
and glides into my own,
a broken corpse-snake
dangling from his bill.
What else can this be
but another love ballad
about the clandestine
arrangements of God?

Pilgrim

Sunset pours into the shattered eyes
of an old farmhouse.
Out front the gravel road bends
around someone else's corn.

A man, burnt red from outdoor labor,
wipes his hands over the belly
of his denim shirt, discovers there
an oily spring oozing from his palms.

The man looks and looks and finally finds
the spot they buried the stillborn—
up near the house, as she'd insisted, so she
could watch the grave from the sitting room.

This: a private affair. The crows above,
in their funeral best, mind their manners,
and the deer dare not creep closer
than the edge of the Hickory wood.

The man kneels near a smooth rock.

When it happened, he took it badly,
refused an equal share in the burden.
There's no making that up to her now.
But he can finally set free some words
he has shouldered these ten-thousand days.

They are good words, but insufficient.
He is grateful, at least, to deliver them
before the mortician picks his pockets
and paints away the craters around
his own window-broken eyes.

Tribute

Go down and tell
them who works
in the lower valley:
the great mother
claims seven fat oxen.
The loggers must numb
their rebel tongues.

Sleeping in the Town of My Birth

is not particularly a comfort
nor an anxiety
most of the time.

Surrounded by the usual joys,
my daughters and wife
snoring beside me,
a third child about the size
of a blueberry in the belly,
the usual worries nonetheless
flash like slasher movie scenes
against my closed eyelids.
Rare cancers, car crashes,
humiliating professional rejections.

And stranger things, too.
Old blues riffs ringing like
invisible church bells.
Something Jim once said
to Huck in the Good Book.

The only real difference here
is the nagging knowledge
that somewhere among
the giant warped Victorians
a man sleeps better than I—
a man who sold to my mother

the Fentanyl patches
she tore open with her teeth
and animal-lapped with her tongue
until her damaged heart went still
one bone-numb winter night
as my father dreamed
his last hopeful dreams
of ever growing happy
beside her.

I am a gentle person, ask around.
I strum a ukulele; I read
to kindergarteners professionally.
But I confess, when not at my best,
I've imagined entering
his bedroom, silent as he snores.
Of covering his eyes, plugging his nose
with thumb and finger,
and pouring her ashes thick
into his gaping mouth-hole,
so he too can know firsthand
the pain of waking at three AM
choking on her memory.

Panic Attack

is what my doctor calls it
when my mind and body
get a twenty-minute divorce,
one continuing to raise the children,
albeit shakily,
while the other flails and thrashes
like some animal
caught in the hunter's rusty trap—
leftovers, of course,
from time out of mind,
the age of constant fight or flight,
but also from a childhood
where flying dishes, police sirens,
and pulled-knife threats
might slice through the silence
of any given midnight.

The savior in this situation
is tiny and pink
and should be taken once daily
with food.

She is a decent god, as gods go,
her tribute merely the top
end of my emotions.
I can live, I tell myself,
with this tempered joy.

I don't have to cry every time
my daughters paint
a three-eyed elephant
or a Starburst sunset.

The worst part? Once, a fine
hermit lived inside me.
Every time I swallow, a few more
of his beard hairs fall out,
scattering to the four winds.
If you look closely into my eyes,
you can still see him
staring out at the world,
processing, in quiet confusion,
from behind the dimmed bulbs
of my medication eyes.

After the Argument

    1.

Everyone you love
sleeps in a quiet room of midnight.
Which is of some comfort,
at least.

    2.

Alone with the words
you should not have said,
you rest your head
against the storm door,
trying to tame your breath.

In the neighbors' window,
pink and green lights,
the Aurora Borealis
of a television talent show
strobing in the darkness.

A gruff-voiced dog
barks his ineloquent warning
to the coyotes in the field
behind the house.

    3.

An uninvited memory:
your mother and father
embrace in a dingy kitchen,
just an hour or so after
she held a serrated knife
to the white of his throat.

In a corner, you
and your baby sister huddle
like broken puppies,
trying to tame the violence
of your sobs.

4.

The moon a round bone
afloat in a black lake.
Time, a knife. Memory, a knife.
Our failures to understand one another—
small blades, every one.

You tell yourself you are better
than what you come from.

You tell yourself that every
couple has it out now and then.

You look up toward
the neighbors' house again.

Christ, you think, there is
no loneliness on earth
like watching someone
watch someone else
try to dance.

Pelicans

A pouch of white pelicans
on the ancient Mississippi,
a hundred or so sailing
delicately over the bones
of sunken steamboats
and their forever-grinning pilots.

I crouch near the river bank,
stare through a cloud of awe
despite the cool April mist.

How strange—to make a fuss
over a creature I've read
would gladly swallow the teeth
from my children's skulls.

I admit it. Something dark
has hunted me a long time now.
No one can see it, but I can
see it, just as I can see the songs
that crawl from a widow's eyes.

A Moment in Kansas

Somewhere in Kansas
a night train torches
through the dark stomach
of the prairie.

The man in the car
on the rural route
turns his head
for just a moment.
He wonders if
he has ever made
his father proud.

But only a moment.
Now he turns from
the disembodied flames.
At the crossroad
he signals left.
The engine hums
the ballad of whatever
comes after.

The Inheritance

1.

There is a photo
of you
in our first few
years together
when we lived
in the woods
and shared meat
with the neighbors

You cradled
a pumpkin
in both arms
like an infant

Your eyes then
were so bright

2.

My mother
had an instinct
for violence

Over the years
I learned
which words

would cause
the cold sting
of her hand
across my face

Then I said them
and said them
just to punish her
with guilt

3.

I was five
when my grandfather
took me out
to the farm
where his brother
slung hay
and led me around
on that
starkissed beauty
of a horse

Grandpa was so
gentle with me
and with the mare
who seemed half
in love
from the way she
nuzzled his hair

and yet

who do you think
taught my mother
to hit?

4.

If I loved you once
for those
bright eyes
I love you more now
for everything
that has made them
a little tired

This is a story
about how
a cycle breaks
about how you
taught me
there are better rivers
in which we can
drown
our ancestors' rage

This is a story
about our confident
daughters
who know nothing

of pain except
the hairbrush through
tough tangles
before bed

As for me—
I know nothing
of what you have
borne
to get us here

But listen: I am
trying

5.

Green fingers
of grass
reach up through late
April snow

A good man
we know
lies unconscious
in the hospital
with a stroke

Our new baby
would have been
about a month old
by now

We walk
the gaudy aisles
of the super center
my hand against
the small of
your back

Our girls alternate
requests for all things
sugar
with questions
about the nature
of God

Here we are

We have
done it

We have
made it

It feels so much
like coming home
when I stop
to press my face
into your hair

Hovland, Minnesota

The girls finally tire of their wild dances.
The sun begins to slide behind the pines.

I sit upon a driftwood throne, watch
waves break white against beach rock.

At the far horizon, sky and water cease
their slight division, melding into a single blue.

Meanwhile, my own mirrors, ages nine and five,
seem to grow a little further from me every day.

But on this night they come in close.
We huddle together in a tattered old quilt,

and I tell them tales of Ole Brunes, the first
immigrant fisherman to build in this bay,

the storms he battled, the cows he sailed
up along the coastline from Grand Marais.

Many others since have fished this rich spot
where the Flute Reed flows into Superior.

They also loved daughters, and they watch now
with a jealousy only the dead have earned.

I feel our impermanence like a wild storm
inside my bones, draw the quilt tighter

against the bluster and chill of the fishermen's
breath blowing off the big lake.

Whatever news they're whispering can be dealt
with later. It is nothing the children need to hear.

The most we can hope for

is that the cock that morning
does not crow,

and the turkey buzzards turn
just a moment from
their afternoon spoils
toward the chime of the church bell,

and in the barrooms that night,
the fractured from across
our wide and dusty county
try their hands at redemption
through recollection,
though their words may prove
no more than frail flowers
tattooed across the shoulders
of the dead.

Maybe, if we are lucky,
someone remembers to read
that Raymond Carver poem
or cue up a lonesome
Hank Williams tune.

And then the March moon
sinks off to sleep
in a fallow cornfield.

And dreaming, she mourns
where only the gospel
plow can reach her.

Storm, Rural Missouri

Though the coming rain
announces itself by rustling
the distant corn,
the barns remain immutable
as weathered grey monks.
Without words, they pray
over the dog who sleeps
forever in his soil bed
beside the oranged relic
of a horse-drawn plow.
On rage the blood sugar wars.
The lust for nicotine continues.
The time-crumpled angels
pull on their Carhartt robes
and stand under wide awnings
as lightning unstitches the sky.
Here, every storm is forty nights
from stating the profound.

Colorado

I sit beneath the first sun,
yards from the cautious mule deer,
and name myself by parts:
the right arm of insignificance,
the left eye that also matters not,
the heart about which
no words need be said.
The mule deer grows easier
with each new erasure
until he finally moves
near enough to touch.
But too late—I have receded
into the mountain crags,
turned memory like morning fog.

Federico Garcia Lorca Blues

These blues are lunar, blues of the moon
and the moonlight and the white spell
the moonlight casts on tree-stubbled hills.

They belong to Andalusia, yet I have seen them too
folk dancing the streets of Chicago in a gale
and smelled them over the insulin bottle
my grandfather tilted every evening
before needling out the potion
that staved off the duke of all shadows.

These are blues that incubate in the eager
throats of scavenger birds latched
to the abandoned silos of the Ozarks.

But most of all, they are the blues of the four
varieties of human sleep--three of them defined,
the fourth still to be discovered.

From *American Ephemeral*

Worried Playground Daddy's Blues

On the playground I strum guitar while my daughter
dangles upside down from the bar above the tall slide,

and inside my middle-aged brain a movie
plays: the pop-art radiance of ambulance lights,

then the cold eye of a weary doctor who rubs
the bridge of his nose and glances back

at the darkly cloaked hospital chaplain
before clearing his throat to speak.

Enough of that, I say. *I don't want you
to hurt yourself.* Trying to sound composed

when what I mean is *I love you please
don't die on me the way my mother did.*

Something about Missouri in November,
the trees so recently vacant of leaves.

That and another bad triglycerides reading
have me on high alert,

but then, I hear we've all gone half-insane
with protectiveness, and I believe it,

can remember how Mom let us roam freely
the trailer park and the thick woods,

how we skipped alongside passing Amtraks,
checking in only for Kool-Aid and ham sandwiches.

God, I wish I could go back, take her by the shoulders,
look her in the eyes and say come on, just pay attention,

not at all for those sweet dangers she permitted us
but because our time was already evaporating.

Oklahoma

Where grown-old pickups go
to live out their remaining days.
The rusty, the crusty, the boxlike in body,
the last of the clunker-cash refugees
parked outside midcentury diners
or near the downest and dirtiest dives—
or else half off the highway, like this F-150,
the powdered blue one with red dirt dusting her hood
and red dirt grubbing up her wheelwells,
the same red dirt on the bootsoles
of the grizzled old cowboy
who wakes in her cab and straightens his hat
and steps gingerly into the hot Oklahoma sun
to the sounds of bone creak and joint pop.
Who two-minute gravel coughs his lungs clear
and leans smoking against her tailgate
as he scans the red dirt horizon for signs
of the invisible pale horse rider.

Begin with a whole boy,

two sea green eyes, ten fingers, and a tangle of dark hair tossed over his forehead. A whole boy with a whole crush on a small girl wearing braces and a rock T-shirt from the early 1970s. Now throw in a drill press and another boy, one who may or may not also have a crush on the small girl. Observation would seem to suggest that she, at least, has a crush on him.

The whole boy pulls down on the drill press lever, shaping wheels en masse for the class's next project, CO_2 race cars for the school derby. He may be working the drill press, but he's watching the small girl and the other boy, and when the two pass in the center of the woodshop and the small girl hands off a note, the whole boy loses half his concentration. There is suddenly a great quantity of blood.

From somewhere inside the mess of blood a thumbnail corkscrews upward, a heap of mottled flesh, a bone that isn't meant to be seen without an X-ray. The whole boy does not seem to notice. In fact, it is only when the shop teacher chokes out a very bad word and wraps the ruined thumb in his paisley necktie that the whole boy finally glances away from the middle of the room, eyes blinking rapidly in confusion.

In some ways, it isn't nearly as bad as it could be. At the hospital the whole boy and his parents learn that every part is still in place, that the scars will eventually heal. He nods as each grown person reminds him just how lucky he is not to have lost a thumb that day, or worse. He nods and seems to agree. Sometimes he even repeats that last word back to the speaker: "Worse." But in truth his mind has never left the woodshop. His mind's eye has never stopped staring into its terrible, tainted center. And in that moment there is nothing anyone can say that will make him believe he can ever be whole again.

In Little League once

after bobbling
a slow bouncer,
I made the mistake
of rolling my eyes
at our coach,
who grabbed my collar
and hissed
his terrible coffee
breath
into my pale face
until I began
to sob and jerk
like a puppet.

When he let go
and turned back
toward
the dugout,
he was forced
to look up
and then
look up again
just to meet
the hard eyes
of the man
whose right hand
had just grabbed
ahold
of his collar.

Hell, I don't
know why
I even told you
that story just now.
I don't condone
collar grabbing,
would prefer
nobody ever grab
anybody's collar
much less do
whatever
comes after that.

I guess part
of me just wishes
every little boy
had one chance
to see his old man
that way.

First Lesson in Meat, 1984

They crash through
the ratty screen door,
all gunflash and colorful
beer cans.
Five men, blood or in-law,
their patchy-bearded
throats alive
with hunter laughter
and gruff guy chatter.
Up front, my grandfather.
Undisputed chief, he holds
the pink thing, the dead
rabbit-flesh thing,
one ear in each of his hands.

These were hands that held me
in my towel after a bath,
comforted me writhing
and screaming at dream demons
in the deepest cricket hours
of the night.
Hands that poured
my milk,
chocolate or white,
and parted my translucent hair,
and tied and delicately retied
my shoelaces after my mother
forbid me Velcro.

These were hands that often
rested so tenderly against
my cheek—
and still they could kill
and cut and rip
the skin from what they'd slayed.
And before they'd even seen
a sink of soapy water,
they would reach out to hold
me again—
still my grandfather's hands
but changed now,
somehow different.
Streaked in pink, washed.
But only in the blood
of their own making.

If only Ken Burns

could get his hands on this footage. Telemachus,
aged eight years, already thickening, athletic
but still uncertain in his movements. The big neighborhood
ballgame against the brutes who would become
known forever as suitors. Third inning,
towering popup to left. T. calls for it
the whole way, but Odysseus snares it barehanded
just inches above the boy's outstretched glove.
Not hard to see how such a move might confirm,
I don't really trust you, son. A boy may spit
into the dirt for consolation, rub at it with his cleated sandal,
but these are the moments that burrow deep,
that fester, only to surface once the boy becomes
a man, armed with a ninety-plus per hour sinker
that dives like a trained falcon -- a gift he honed alone
chucking rocks against rocky hillsides during long
and fatherless summers beneath the white Ithacan sun.

Odysseus. Broken king. PTSD. Bone-heavy, slower now
of wit and reflex, already an hour or two deep
into his cups. Does he understand his son's words
carry more of a threat now than an entreaty?
In his hands the prince carries two weather-beaten
lumps of broken cow-leather. *Hey, Pops,* he says,
what say you and me have a quick game of catch?
And he holds the gloves out, not quite in offering.

Barn Jamboree, Rosine, Kentucky

Sunset slants its salmon light
through the open doors.
A man, whom we're told
has recently (and only just barely)
survived the bypassing
of multiple arterial blockages
by a hotshot surgeon
down in Bowling Green,
accepts a battered house Martin,
takes the stage to perform here
for the first time in many months.

He adjusts the microphone,
toys with the tuners,
glances around the twilit barn nervously,
finally nodding at the audience
seated on long benches like church pews.
But before he can begin
a lovely woman about his age
sidles up from the side, surprising him.
She gives him a look that seems to ask
if there's any chance of a duet,
and you don't have to be local
to work out that there's been
some history between them.

Enough so that when he picks
out the first notes
and begins to strum "Waltz Across Texas,"
their voices entwine, naturally,
like the fingers of the old
couples who stand and press close
and sway together
only a little more carefully
than they must have fifty-odd years ago
when this song and their love
were both newborn to the world.

Joy is a complicated matter;
it almost never arrives crystalline.
I have seen it bloom
even on the faces of broken men
buying cheap beer on the odd
Tuesday in November,
unmistakable but muddied up always,
mixed with a hint of guilt or resignation.
The singing man's face is like that.
So is the lady's.
You can see they are doing something
they once believed
they might never do again
and now must consider
what other dreamghosts
they might yet sing life into.

The tune is like any other tune,
and soon enough it shuffles toward an end.
But her fingers find his shoulder,
and a silent conspiracy ensues
to strum on and reprise the chorus
once, and then twice more,
as if they are terribly afraid
for the sound to stop,
afraid to step out from behind
the sweet safety of perhaps.

And then they must, and do.

The bow, the wave, the decision:
all arrive together in an instant.
She leaves him with a kiss on the cheek
that brings high color to his face,
floats out with the applause
into the soft Kentucky twilight.

The rest of the evening he can be seen
slouching, exhausted, near the back
entrance to the barn
as the regular band swings, western-style.
Every so often he runs his hand
absently over the area of his chest
where beneath his plaid shirt I imagine
must live one hell of a scar
from all this business with his heart.

First Lesson in Ephemerality

My grandfather bought his burial plot early,
tucked away in a small country cemetery
adjacent to a sturdy old corn-and-cows farm.

From his chosen spot, the soft green hills
rolled off toward a far horizon, and beyond
that a mysterious land in which he believed

he'd someday live, perhaps even settle
unless the sum deeds of his life meant
the final judgement went another way.

But he must have thought too of the shell
he'd be leaving behind, laid up under
all that heartland sod and soil indefinitely,

since he'd planted a tree like those found
back in his native Kentucky so that he might
rest again in the shade he'd loved as a boy.

This weekend we watched thirty-year-old
home VHS tapes, all the people in them now dead
in one sense or another, though some sat

right next to me on the sofa as the video
wobbled and blinked in and out, going dark
and fuzzy every fifteen or twenty seconds.

I don't mean this critically. We all die
a number of times before we cease biologically,
each change a small stepping-stone death

on the way up to the big dark leap into the empty;
even this poem will have died many times
before meeting your critical or sympathetic eye.

On these home movies I heard my grandfather's voice
before it had gone rough and world-weary,
before the slow death of its youth and vigor.

In one tape, he narrated a walk through his garden,
in the next he sang old Carter Family songs,
in a third he called out, teasing his eldest, my mother.

My mother's grave is near to my grandfather's.
On her headstone, my father's name, the dates
marking his lifespan already half carved, waiting.

Dad says he regrets having it made this way, and me--
I suppose I regret my crimes against the spirit
of what I purport to stand for, believe in.

Our regrets are most resistant to small deaths;
they habitate in us like household ghosts
until our houses finally burn down or collapse.

Listen: here I wanted to return you to the cemetery,
to tell you something about the breeze there
on certain warm afternoons, but I just can't

seem to stop touching everything around me—
memorizing all matter as it exists on this particular day
through fingertips, through palms or cheeks.

Here's an orange. Here is a guitar. Here, my father's
big shoulders. This is my daughter's' tiny hand.
This: a book. These: the soft hairs on my wife's neck.

And this: today's fleeting version of my face.

The Farmers at Their Morning Coffee

Hear what news passes their lips
between the slow, ginger sips
from steaming plastic cups
at the local Hardee's.

Hear the coded odes
to past courting prowess,
the ballads of Mesozoic-like fish
caught not by pole but old-fashioned
Lincoln-style wrestling.

Uniformed in shirtsleeves
and meshback feedcompany hats,
they tell of coon dogs
treeing iguanas, old flood stories
to rival Gilgamesh or the Bible.

They tell in hushed voices
of witchwives who watch and hear
from afar the truth of a man's heart.

Was another pitiful year
for the crops, says one.
Too wet to plant in the spring
and too dry to grow
in the summer, says another.
This one's circulatory piping
has clogged up again.

And now the cold, too, has returned.
They all agree it really is
the deep kind that settles
into earth and old bones alike.
Things are always just a little
bit worse than they were
this time yesterday morning.

Still, it must feel good to be
so old and alive on this frosty morning,
to drink such hot coffee
and perhaps pick over
a rubbery breakfast platter
while curing the literal truth
of its shameful lack of color
here at this table where all the seats
are filled for only God
knows how much longer.

Arthur and Marie, 1961

Late autumn now, Illinois. The trees, half-dead,
wave their gnarled arms above the bone
white gravel of the rural country road

down which he steers the old rustbucket flatbed,
her nose toward the pinkish twilight, toward a town
where they'll meet his folks for supper.

The day has been a long one, full of harsh fieldwork
and minor disagreements that kept them from sharing
they've both been dreaming of a child again.

Now he is sorry and she is ready to let him be,
and so his hand bridges their space, finding her cheek
for a sweet second before shooting back to the wheel.

At the far reach of their headlights, a great ghostlike bird--
a snowy owl, perhaps, though rare around here.
It sits in stony stillness between the drying cornfields.

Consider the intricacies of human recollection.
If she is, in fact, with child, they will one day turn
this vision into an omen, even making an angel

of its wide white wings and its sudden skyward ascension,
everything electric with importance--their shallow breath
as they watch, eyes wide and unblinking, the way

their hands find each other and interlock on her knee.
Just as true is the opposite--the bird becomes the angel
of death if what's stirs in her is instead malignant.

But if she is empty, except for her basic dissatisfaction,
then the vision astonishes only for that brief instant.
Once it is gone, it is, truly and finally, gone.

In fact, trees, road, twilight, autumn, corn: all gone,
the whole scene blended into the dense camouflage
of memory, forgotten fifteen years, then twenty more,

until even that cells-deep desire for a child of their flesh
is lost to them, buried beneath her kindly cynicism,
barred behind his stoic, even-if-my-back's-broke will.

Forgotten so long it is left, finally, to the storyteller's invention.
Buried so deep when the dust is finally blown off
they can only imagine it a fiction that never existed at all.

Farmer, Clutching Chest

The circumstance of his death is nigh.
But as luck would have it, this tragedy
is not without heart; it has gone out ahead
to build an afterlife for him.
Now it stands, silhouetted against a far sunset,
arms raised, waving. The farmer can't see
that far but he imagines his death is smiling.
It wants to know if this is the right place,
this sad plot that seems so much like the harsh
lands he'll soon be leaving.
Yes, he nods, *that's the place.* He can hardly wait.
He wants to gather all that good soil
in his fingers, to horde it to himself.
He wants all of it: the inelegance of pig stench
and the garble of good tires treading on gravel road.
Doesn't he understand it will be hard?
He understands, wants it that way. Is he supposed to
ask for some sort of hoity-toity heaven?
Hell, that's all he's ever known is survival,
and he must know if he can do it there, too--
in the afterlife, where the cruel wind draws itself
from old testament sources,
and where the unimaginable drought of eternity
will press constantly against the green edges
of all he dares to grow.

Old Men Laughing on a Park Bench in Early October

One grips the iron armrest; the other clutches a fedora from a distant past. Both shake and shake and shake. Their eyes stretch wide. The inner wells from which they draw their joy must be deeper than any I've witnessed in my short life. Watching, I forget for a moment the reason I am even sitting here, and who I believe is to blame. The three of us, and the dew glittering diamondlike on the grass, and the first few vibrant leaves of fall—for a moment we don't seem to belong to the world of solid things. But eventually, the laughter does sputter to a stop, and the silence in its wake is so heavy and total by contrast, it is like a preview of the great long silence to come. Perhaps the old men recognize this, too, because after a minute, one of them—the one with the fedora—grins, shakes his head slowly and repeats the inciting word again: *curtains*. But of course: nothing this time, no reaction from either of them. The moment's magic is all used up. It is right about then that I look over my shoulder and discover my bad news tromping through the grass. He holds his head high and I can hear him whistling his lonesome train-whistle whistle as he approaches, a violent whistle, a whistle that rips through the laughter-less quiet without conscience. I am on the tracks, and I think to myself, *What can I do, what, honestly, can I do, but rise and turn my face and wait to meet whatever may be coming?*

First Lesson in Vietnam, 1987

It was how you stood on your trailer roof
all that sweltering Independence Day, caped
in a threadbare flag of our nation, encircled
by Budweiser empties, plates of burning incense.
It was how you stood there and also how,
lit from above by those colorful celebration
bombs, you made me believe in the myth
of the romantic savage. I had no idea then
what you'd tried to accomplish alone
in the toolshed with the extension cord,
nor how, in a few years, you'd be hauled in—
armed robbery, just days after the first
Gulf War broke out. I saw only your hair,
shoulder length, and your scarred torso
bare and bony, home to a tattooed menagerie
of fantasy creatures: elf, dragon, phoenix,
centaur, faerie, citizens of a land
to which you'd gladly defect. It was all that,
and it was how recklessly you lit
bottle rockets and fired them from your
hollowed-out walking stick. And it was how—
finally—when my father cupped his hands together
and shouted, *Hey, Chuck, give it a rest, guy.*
It's getting pretty late, you turned, delicate
as a dancer in the shimmering moonlight,
and offered him what little was left
of your mangled middle finger.

I Take Forty-Five Minutes to Shoot a Portrait of My Father

My father standing here
now leaning over there
now turning his patient face
left and then right.

Tilting his bearded chin
according to my instruction.

Grinning at an old joke
I've raked up from our past
to crinkle his eyes
and soften his expression.

This posing is real work for him
but no complaints—
the old man is of a certain generation
and he understands effort
as a brand of broad currency
that can mean good faith
to business partners or employers
and to a lover can mean
that long-awaited shedding
of the selfishness
that shells us all in our youth.

Here it means a mere portrait
can transform into the words
I want but fail to speak.

Weeks later, when I finally
give him this print
matted and framed in barnwood
I will give to him himself
precisely the way I see him.

And the effort spent will read
like a personal inscription
scrawled not onto the back
of the photograph itself
as might be the custom
but directly into the soft meat
that makes my father's heart.

Playing Blues Harp Alone in an Unfinished Basement

At a ballgame once,
I saw a great hero
with comic book biceps
launch three home runs
of gargantuan distance.
He circled the bases
more slowly each time,
as if perhaps he grasped
just how fleeting
his greatness would be--
but no, I believe he meant
to embarrass the pitcher,
a renowned and arrogant
goateed villain
who liked to fill
the daily news with
the legend of himself.

That hero fell, of course,
and to such depths
that a common stooge
such as myself
can now feel justified
in pitying him—
and I do pity him,
not for losing greatness

but for having ever
borne it at all.
You see, once a person
has reached the pinnacle,
he can never again
find any real pleasure
in being well and truly inept.

I'm glad there's
no chance I'll ever
ascend to greatness.
I prefer to know
how sweet it feels
on a stray Saturday
in late April, let's say,
the wife and the baby
off in town, visiting,
plenty of cold beers
stacked in the fridge,
to toss the drywall knife
on top of the unopened
bucket of joint compound
and drop the needle
on Howlin' Wolf instead.

I know we're not allowed
to admit such scandals,
but every now and again
I *like* to be reminded
most of what we do

doesn't really matter.
I like that I can
simply close my eyes
and blow along
with boozy conviction
and even see the humor
a few minutes later
when I discover my
suppose'd best friend
and confidant the dog
has once again buried
her head deep in the laundry
piled in the corner.

Late August

All that summer the trailer park baked beneath the cruelest sun in recent memory. A drought year. The slender grass strips serving as backyards yellowed before slowly achieving a pale brown color, a texture strawlike and crunchy underfoot. Where grass would not grow the dry dirt cracked and ant armies crawled up from jagged gaps in long black trains, scouting out dropped popsicles, discarded hot dogs, open trash cans. Everywhere was heard the rumbling hum of window AC units, of laughing children, dirt-faced, tongues Kool-Aid red, small bellies full of cold ham sandwich. Here and there sat the elderly streetside in woven lawn chairs or on yard swings, sipping golden sweet tea. Against the logic of the heat they wore long pants and sleeves and did not sweat. In other driveways shirtless men hunched over the engines of rusted jalopies, barking long curse strings as if to invoke the secret language of automobile resurrection. Their blue, gylphlike tattoos hid in the shade of the car hoods but revealed their mysterious selves when the men stood upright and lit cigarettes and rolled their shoulders and leaned far forward and then far backward to stretch stiff muscles while contemplating the dysfunction hidden within the guts of these machines.

Someone somewhere on this street or the next cooked meat over a charcoal flame, or so smell would indicate. A boy stood atop a dumpster at the head of the road, face tilted upward to the sun as he drained a bottle of orange soda in four or five loud gulps. The trailers themselves with their faded paint, with their shades liked closed eyelids, appeared ill or even passed out sleeping. Five or six weeks rolled on, days and nights identical in their slow-spinning relentlessness. One afternoon, a fat purple storm cloud

approached but blew by without relinquishing a single raindrop. The tease of it must have been too much. That afternoon, two neighbors, the war veteran and the carpenter, altercated over borrowed money, prescription pills, a woman they both believed they could own. But it turns out they were mistaken.
A knife blade appeared, mirroring back the white daylight. There came an animal grunt. Later, near where her car had been parked, the dark stain on the gravel driveway told another chapter of the story.

Marriage (Detail)

She wakes me unexpectedly
in the dead of the night,
panicked, breathing hard,
asking, 'Is she talking to me,
is she talking to me?'
'Who?' I say.
"The doll," she says. "The *doll*."
Then immediately begins
to snore again, leaving me alone
to contemplate that
while staring into the darkness.

Children in the Middle Ages

Earlier that night, a middle-aged man dressed himself in a cape and green tights and shimmied up a tree to rescue his neighbor's new kitten. We sat numbly over our steaming hamburger pie, watching first the climbing oil prices and then the live feed as our would-be hero lay in a twisted heap on the sidewalk at the base of the tree, his neck in fifty shattered pieces, blood fleeing his faulty skull in astonishing haste. In the dining room, us, meaning: you, me, and the sick child whose cough occasionally ripped across the newscaster's flat Midwestern cadence. After dinner, you were supposed to be reading her a book about children in the middle ages, the games they played, but you kept looking up at the television. This was not a good time in our marriage, though it was perhaps a little better a time than now, at least. I don't suppose you remember how you turned, or how we looked at one another for a handful of seconds? I thought we were speaking to each other without words, a secret language of understanding. You thought I was being weird. Eventually, one of us must have found the remote and changed the channel. Or maybe we just turned the TV off. That is where the silence begins in my memory, and I have yet to come to the other side of it. It is a sound so loud and terrible, I'm not even sure you can hear me trying to tell you this now.

Museum Guard's Blues

There was this old man and he always wore a blues player's fedora, just like the one I liked to wear. He would cry in front of the romantic landscapes in a way that made you want to hold his hand. The walls and the ceiling were transparent. Outside, you could see when the thunderstorms were gathering with menacing intent.

The president at this time was a person history would not remember with kindness. A know-it-all woman stood in a shadowy corner, passing on spurious information about the French and Indian War. There were dozens of mournful sculptures from different historical eras. To me they all seemed to be wailing in a single voice. I had something like thirty dollars in my bank account and I was crazy in love with a performance artist who played classical music badly on purpose. I didn't get it and she refused to explain.

Sometimes I would look down at my own fingers in the cloudy dishwater or resting in my lap and they would seem to me the most foreign objects. They were capable of doing things, even if I was not. I would pick up the guitar and they would find the chords even when my mouth could not find the words. My fingers never seemed to care. They were of their own mind.

I had a child somewhere back there in my past but his mother put him up for adoption. I believe she would have made a damn good mother. I'd lived in three states in the past year alone but none of them had felt anything like a final destination. I have to wonder about people who think they have it all figured out and will even tell lies about the French and Indian War just to prove it to their own fearful hearts. The museum had once been my place of refuge. Now it just made me think about the history of my own misdeeds. I could see that the paintings hung along the walls were just a long, pretty documentation of an eternity of lies. I knew nobody would ever remember me after I was gone. It was a comfort to think this way.

I wanted to quit picking the guitar, to let my fingernails grow long and twisted like this man whose picture I'd seen once in a book. I wanted to do a kindness for someone and watch from a distance as they felt grateful toward a stranger. My father once told me that the real measure of a man is his ability to grant forgiveness for all things. I wanted to believe that. Especially since my nose has always been a little crooked on my face because of him.

Three days driving through scrubby desert
and semi-arid mountain,

ducking the stern southwestern sun within the walls
of old adobe missions Socorro County north.
Today, a mission somewhere on the high road to Taos--
my seven-year-old daughter's patience for quiet places
breaks down entirely. She bounces from teal
flip-flop to teal flip-flop, whining she's *tired of Jesus
dying all over everywhere like this.*

At the mention of Jesus the three-year old begins
to drum her Tinkerbell-shirted belly.
Hey, Daddy, Daddy, she wants to know, *was Jesus tough?
Well, well, well, did he have magic power?*
And now the clouds empty.
Do Native Americans believe how Muslims believe?
asks the older girl. *Did Jesus die because he was mad at God?*
wonders the younger.

And so on. My wife and I take turns answering as best we can,
suddenly aware of the misunderstandings
our tiny, Midwest-cornfield existence has already weaved
into their worldview. While they process
all the new information, I study this ancient sanctuary,
adorned with solemn, staring statuettes, consider each
cruel station of the cross, nearly in tears trying to reconcile
the tremendous awe I always feel in houses of God
even twenty years after quitting my childhood church

over a dinosaur dispute with the probability this mission
was a factory of forced faith.

And then one more question cuts into my consciousness—
Daddy, are we Christians? Followed by the sound
of the mission doors swinging softly shut.
I breathe in. Look up at the wooden Mother and around
at a few other pilgrims who have wandered in behind us.
Even she, even they seem to be leaning forward,
leading with cupped ears, eager for an answer.

First Lesson in The Dead

--The Museum of International Folk Art, Santa Fe, NM

Wide blue sombrero haloing
                           grim and fleshless grin
while slim skeleton fingers
                           survey fret and string.
Across the wide aisle
                           carved angels ascend

like mariposas, like butterflies,
                           on pretty painted wings.
My preschool daughter
                           simply does not care,
only moves her ear
                           closer, as if trying to hear
what words the tiny
                           bone man sings.

Payphones in the Underworld

My best friend texts me
a picture of a letter my mother
sent him the year she died.

He had forgotten about it
and wants to know whether
I want it for myself?

But the power isn't so much
in the ownership.
It arises from the surprise
in seeing the long loops
of her letters unexpectedly,
how they seem to carry the very
sound of her voice.

The dead know these things.
At just the right moment
they leave off from doing
their secret dead doings
and find a payphone, fish around
for change deep in the pockets
of their burial suits.

The call comes through
and on this end I pass a Camaro
just like the one Mom
rose hell with when we were kids.

Or the V.C. Andrews novels
stacked at the community yard sale
resurrect in my mind the rhythm
of her breathing as she read
evenings by yellow lamplight
in our smoky trailer.

But it's no use calling them.
The dead almost never answer.
You only tie up the line
as they stand patiently by,
tapping bony fingers to skulls
and waiting for the ringing to stop
so they know for certain
the need for reminder has ripened.

From *Lessons in Ruin*

From the Poet

Friend, I have only stopped in
to briefly describe for you

the bushbrowed old German,
and the way he wrestled

that ancient squeezebox
into a slow swerving polka—

music for the barefoot widow
to dance away the grief

she'd long hidden behind
eyes half-painted like two

deserted roadside attractions.
And maybe to add a line or two

about the shadow that seemed
to rise from her skin like vapor,

leaving behind some other
more hopeful being entirely.

I might even say something
of the after-embrace—strangers,

before and after, holding on
hard to ward off the end of times.

But then—back to my own house.
Someone I've hurt is waiting.

The Boy From Stanford, Illinois (Population 670) Sees the Van Gogh

Just *look* at that, he said.
   Makes me want to run
my fingers all over it like
   blind people writing.

You mean Braille? said a man.

The museum guard chuckled.

And the boy chuckled, too,
   knowing full well
she couldn't stand there and
   guard him forever.

Bird on a Wire, 1989

you know, I never have forgotten
that pretty blueish-black bird
perched high on the telephone wire
near the entrance to the trailer park
nor the baseball I kept hurling
from down in the scorching street
just to see if I had that kind of aim

I did not, but the bird certainly did

with astonishing precision he dropped
his wet white warning onto my
forehead and into my gaping mouth
before fluttering off for friendlier climes

and all the way home the other children
and even a few adults
laughed at me, made clever remarks
such as *hey, you look like a bird
just shit on your face*
and *haha, did your face just get shit on
by some kind of a bird?*

and me coughing and hacking,
bawling and swatting at my mouth
with the back of my mitt,
mind full of scarlet and murder

some days I'm sure I must have
learned a godly lesson that afternoon—
about kindness, humility, the golden rule,
some wisdom that bettered me forever
and allows me to be a stronger husband,
a gentler and more generous father,
to contribute more to society

but most days I just wish
my control had been
just a little bit better

Hooky Bobbers, 1992

There were two of them
my uncle to be
and his younger brother.
Hard to remember
if they were drunks
already, or only still
drunks in training.
But I'll never forget
after those big snows
the way they'd slide
on slick bootsoles
through the streets
of our trailer park
crouched low, clinging
to the rear bumper
of a roaring '76 Bronco
at thirty or even forty
miles per hour.

Can you understand
how badly I wanted
their idiotic grace
in taming useless challenges?
How badly I wanted
people to shake their heads
and roll their eyes at me—
but then secretly grin
at my mad badboy antics?

Well, I did. I wanted
to toss away my
statebought glasses
and join in the stupidity
to slide and drink
and drink and drink
and when the beers
had finally added up
and I lost my grip
coming around a corner
and wound up
sprawled out and broken
in somebody's yard
I wanted more than anything
not to learn my lesson
but to laugh a deep
deep immortal laugh
and then to start making
wobbly angels in the snow.

Sunrise Subterfuge (in the first person)

At six a.m.
he enters my bedroom
a massive hulk
of hardened laborer
all stubblefaced
all flannelclad and frowny
all stooped over
from the sheer weight
of fatherhood and failure
but already
I have my speech
prepared:

'I *could* work' I say
'but don't you think
the cruel Midwest has
asked too much
of its men already—
has called it weak
and unbecoming even
for a man to give himself
over to tender emotion?'

He blinks.

'One ought' I say
'pursue softer things

as a rule
and two softer things
in close proximity
ought pursue one another.'

He scratches his jaw
and blinks.

'For honestly' I say
 'who can love an anvil,
an anchor tender or tenderly
and tell me old man
is not the heart itself
as a thing rather squishy?'
'But be assured
this back of mine

it too will break
this hopeful spirit
it too will rot
like so many tiny
factory towns in shambles
all around us'

Blink scratch blink. Cough
cough.

'Old man' I say
'believe you me
there is no reason
for anyone to hurry.'

To which as ever
he says nothing—
then as now
just blink scratch blink
cough cough cough
and not even a whispered
curseword betrays
his disappointments
as deep as the pockets
of the rich men we'd serve
but never become
each of us
for a different reason.

The Best Friend's Lament

Twenty-nine miles from Nowhere
to East Nowhere, Missouri. Dead
of winter. Windblind, letterjacketless.
Rattling around the back
of a drunken farmboy's pickup.
Nose to nose with the frozen
carcass of yesterday's buck.
And all because the girl
at the end of this rural route
has a parent-empty house
and the right sort of prairie
sadness in her eyes.

We all know the way
this old ballad goes. The cast
of white headlamps around
the sharp country bend.
The heavy sheriff crunching
through the hard mud rows
of a frost-marbled field.
Everything eerie beneath
the blood-red sunrise.

But I swear
it would never end

with a mother cradling
an old baseball trophy
like an infant.

Not if they made me God
of the Middle West.

At Sixteen

The Midwest belches
from its smokestacks
beside the churning river
and all of its fathers stretch
bleary eyed and bitter
about their swollen
father ankles
their crooked
father fingers
their click-clacking
father joints
and their endless
father mortgages
while a room away
their beardless sons
nurse black eyes
nurse hangovers
roll out of beds
and into coveralls
unknowingly rolling
into their fathers' skins
and their fathers' troubles
but the black sheep
reads Boethius to the spiders
by flashlight
beneath the stairs
weeps for everything

worth weeping for
in a place where weeping
is forbidden
feels himself becoming
in a place where becoming
is also forbidden—
a place where only
the smokestacks belching
the river churning

and the gentle turning
of son to father
and son to father
have yet to be forbidden

That Morning As We Slept in Our First House Together

there came a strange
percussion
which in my dream I took
for the glad ringing
of my father's hammer
the old man busy
constructing homemade toys
for the cousins
or cradles for all
the new babies
as I slept in late
on those sweet sweet
Saturday mornings.

Which I suppose is why
it was such a surprise
to wake
and stretch
to leave you curled
like a question mark
atop the sheets
and pry open the blinds
and find
not that melon-hearted
man at work
for the children he loved

but rather
a police officer's hand
rising and falling
again and again
in the soft light
of sunrise
as he hammered joyfully
the meth head's
mangled face
into the rusted hood
of our Chevy Cavalier.

Goodbye, Sancho Panza

I meet
a Slim Jim munching
Sancho Panza
goateed now
all leathered out
and in close contact
with his inner beast

Five hundred years
after the death
of his beloved mule
he rides a Kawasaki
wants to know if I will
sally forth with him
through Missouri
as his loyal
dimwit squire

There's this broad
he's s'pposed to meet
near the riverside in Cape
he explains

So I pull out my blues harp
and toot a few notes
while I think of the baby
my sweet scented daughter
whose pudgy upturned nose
matches my own

A newborn's a fragile thing
a soft cooing heap
of possibly maybe
long before it hardens
into something permanent
like a soul
and for the first three weeks
I refused to use her name

Earlier tonight I drank
to overcoming these fears
to Jesus and science
and green bean casserole
but Sancho is as sober
as an ice cube
as serious as any
grain of sand
and despite the longing
I'm forced to decline

Missouri is veined with
deep winding caverns
so many of her secrets
tightly concealed
and anyway I'm
too old and civilized
for the sort of digging
it would take
to learn anything good

The Flour Epiphany

This morning, I decide I want
to make biscuits the proper way,
flour and Crisco and buttermilk
all meted out in careful measure,
but there is an accident
involving the flour canister;
a white mushroom cloud rises,
coats my hair,
my eyebrows and bare shoulders,
and I cough and hit my head on a cabinet
and say I word I won't repeat
in case my baby daughter
ever reads this poem.

When I examine myself,
angling my scalp lightward,
staring hard into the bathroom mirror,
this sprinkled-over look plays tricks
and I see my father in two versions:
one as a young man,
when he wore so much drywall dust
with a vast, innocent dignity,
and one as an old, old man,
when the color will be nothing
more than another dreaded sign
of his accumulated age

And I ask myself out loud
is it really so wrong to want
to hold certain things
while your grip is still strong
rather than wait until whatever
you might wish to hold
is too heavy for old man hands
and only keeps falling away
soon as your swollen fingers
can close in around it.

Illinois Route 3

If this road could answer
I would ask her what it is like
to follow the path
of the rippleshimmery river
for too many miles
through the slowly ghosting towns
and the corncovered landscapes
of the dying Midwest
first through hills so subtle
they seem like mere rumors
and then through more
significant undulations
rising up suddenly
like tumors— only to be abandoned
completely spent and alone
in some lesser Cairo
long before you could ever tune
your ear to the lovely blue notes
of Memphis, Tennessee
or feel the tingling creepies
drifting out from the voodoo
niches of New Orleans

I would kneel down right here
where the darkness is thickest
and hides the sign that warns
Danger: Falling Rock

and I would listen as the one
tiny swath of pavement
glowing brightest white
under the sharp cuticle moon
speaks of its great envy
and the river pageants past
like so many onetime lovers
all arrogant momentum
all callous purpose
without the slightest
hint of hesitation

One More Moon

An evening bursting with corny charm—
a polka band in the park, the bandleader's
terrible jokes about cheerleaders
and divorce court, about rural Arkansas.
Our firstborn, off making allies
or enemies at the foot of the slide.
Her baby sister asleep in the great big
canopied stroller, light blanket draped
overtop to keep away the mosquitos.
The sun dips behind the tree line,
the temperature suddenly more bearable.
You reach for my hand and I don't
recoil exactly, but neither do I accept
your teasing finger gentle over my knuckles.
Tomorrow, it is you who will turn
from my apology and close an invisible
window between us. This too is my fault.
I could place my hand beneath your hair,
 could trace into your neck the secret
code we've written for *please forgive me i forgive you*.
My heart is willing but the back
of my brain still clenches and throbs
with the kick of self-righteous resentment.
August, and another lovely moon rises
over our small town and its empty factory,

where once so many bricks were made
 for building the solid things in this world.
One more moon, and I wonder how
many more before I finally get this right?

To Charlie

If I give you a single rose
the hyperbolic red

of a cartoon fire engine
and I ask you to carry

that red rose all herky-jerky
through the hoodlum-

lined streets of your
monochrome cineverse

and if the lovely dame
removes her flapper hat

and accepts that red rose
and her eyebrows arch

upward in question
and your tongue awakens

and like a perfect baby
you begin to shape your

mouth around "l" and "o,"
you should stop right there.

My God, don't speak, Charlie.
Don't you ever say a word.

Far better if you freeze
just like that, forever

in a moment untarnished
by all the unavoidable

clumsiness of our language,
that first, best word still

unsullied by what lives
outside the human heart.

Elegy for Sounds Forgotten

There is a theory, claims a recent TV show, that words
may live inside the artifacts of the distant past, ghost
vernaculars cut into the details of a vase or a bowl,
what the potter sang or said working wet clay at his
wheel. And this possibility, like so much else, sends
one man tunneling back into his own sacred notions,
causes him to wonder about the lies and truths we all
must say to survive—how these spectral recordings,
were we to unlock them, might contain nothing
of these lies or truths, but only laughter long, long
forgotten.

This is something the man does from time to time.
He crawls down into an invented notion of what
used to be, the same way he crawls into Clarence
Ashley's clawhammer banjoing or curls up inside
Billie Holiday's reedy cooing, and when his wife calls
out to him from the next room over, the only sound
he can distinguish is the sound of his own internal
mechanics processing the dead.

Later he sits in the dark of the present moment, the
future flickering like some star raging at an impossible
distance, and he feels sick over marriage verbiage
carved into their years, words which someday
someone may find in some old thing of theirs, words
he might better remember if only he'd been listening.

Afterpoem

it is not the loss itself that is cruel
thinks the broken man to himself

his teeth tearing wolflike
into his wife's lacy pillows—

only this godforsaken sun,
vengeful and swollen with menace

coming at his window every morning
with its terrible new agenda

a giant cellmate or some relentless
heavyweight champ

Just Before Sleep

The pedigrees of ancient wood,
the hollow ring of the convicted hammer.

Wire hands or borrowed ears,
those you were born with or those grown later on.

People who can name all the prairie flowers.
People who find themselves loving mannequins.

The sound of gunfire before
Yellow, or yellowness, stretched out thin

A long conversation, another failure
Understanding the volume of infinity.

Deer hunters.
Romantic reconciliation.

One mistake and then another relived and relived
again in the holy hereafter.

Or else forgiven and forgotten before
it ever comes to that.

In Case You Were Wondering

what I was thinking
that blazing afternoon in August
when suddenly I put down
my book
and looked over at you leaning
elbows on the porch rail
fitter and wiser and infinitely
more patient
than when you were twenty-two.

I was overcome in that moment
with all you'd become
and I wondered if you felt the same
way about me
and my heap of books
on blind bluesmen and manners
in 17th century France
or if you secretly liked me
better when I was younger
and spoke in that big
foolish beer voice
that carried and made people laugh
two rooms over
and I tried in all sincerity
to hunt the wild turkey
armed only with a laundry sack
and the charm of all the things
I didn't know.

Acclimation

Before I grew used to it
I would wake to the sound
of the Amtrak whistle
echoing down along the tracks
behind our trailer park
and wonder who was hurtling where
through the dark night and across
this wide Illinois prairie
and why and with whom else
and for how long.

But this was before I grew used to it
and to the wind chimes
dangling from the front porch
and to the dogs barking
or fighting in the street
and to the occasional car engine
coughing to life at an unlikely hour.
The laughter of teenagers
up to the best sort of no good,
their stereos pumping neon bass lines
into the black promise of the night.
This was back when
those stark graveyard hours were a time
I could still be startled
into discovering something profound.

Every year now I feel more convinced
it is no good
all this getting used to things.
Mornings, my wife asks me how I slept
and I tell her, *Fine, fine.*

Even I'm not sure what I mean.

The Everyday Parade

But of course the damned old
pickup won't start again,
and they miss the marching bands
in their bright uniforms,
the Shriners tiny in their go-karts,
the waving Santa and the hailstorm
of Dum-Dums and Laffy Taffys.
So next morning he calls
them both in sick,
no loading the fish trucks today,
none of that endless tracing
of loopy letters on wide-ruled paper.
She helps him swap out
the fuel pump
for one from the junkyard
delivered by goateed uncle
on motorbike,
and all afternoon they sit uptown,
a pair of grease-stained gearheads
in the white sunshine,
watching the long slow procession
of the Everyday Parade:
The mother who waits
until her daughter leaves
the restaurant
to light a secret cigarette,
the old men through the window

of the bridal shop
telling with animated hands
what must be jokes or whoppers.
Three stray dogs locked
in tight formation,
the mangiest and most
loyal-looking mutts ever
to slink along a stretch of city street.
A beerkeg hauled
by big enthusiastic boys
in shorts and grimy ballcaps
from truckbed to duplex door.
And finally, not St. Nicholas
but a gangly old splotch-faced drunk
tripstepping up 4th Street
and crooning Sinatra from under
his Victorian mustache,
singing just the way a catfish might,
if he believed no one
could possibly hear his notes
swimming or sinking flat
beneath the spread and weight
of all that muddy water.

First Lesson in Ruin

Abandoned brick factory,
gridded windows shattered
in tic-tac-toes.
Parking lot signs leaning,
gilded in bright orange rust.

Shredded white rose
of historic sale barn,
forgotten, loved briefly
by community fundraiser.
Soon enough: forgotten again.

Bankrupt gas station,
grown over with God's own
golden grasses.
Hideous turkey vultures
latched to tin shed
teetering near rotwood fence.

Little one, I present to you
Missouri, land of your birth.
We have no pyramids here,
no stirring Greek temples.
But we too have our echoes.

Always remember these quiet
tours through her landscape.

And remember them most of all
when your daddy finally crumbles
into a grim reminder of a man.

Poem For Saturday

It was just one of those days
when the philosophy came easy
as whistling in the shower
and every doorway I stepped through
was a metaphor.

Early September and already
a few leaves turning to rust.
Seemed like a good day to wonder
why nobody ever taught me
how to tie my own necktie.
Like a good day to send a message
to all the people I love
in the afterlife
and unpack my warehouse of blessings
one silent thank-you at a time.
To shoot photos of empty park benches
beneath half-open windows
cut into buildings on the brink of collapse.

If ever there was a day, friend,
to fish and catch nothing
but the glint of sunlight on your hook
and a few slippery notions about living,
then what I'm telling you, this day was it.

And I did it. I did it all.

But most of all, what I did was
I refused to be hurried.
In fact, I was about as efficient
as the process of erosion,
and when I came home,
in late afternoon, and happy
as a lit lamppost,
I did not once touch that book
in which the overdegreed genius
informs us that consciousness,
that the *human soul,*
is no more than grand illusion.

Instead I spent the evening
caring only for the loveliness
of my wife's hair tucked behind her ears
and the almost imperceptible music
of my little daughter's sneakers
swishing through the beautiful
high unruly backyard grass
I've no plans of mowing anytime soon.

The Last Year on the Farm

You found your grandfather, remember,
    staring through two rheumy eyes
and two panes of clouded glass
    at an ancient International Harvester,
rusted beyond orange, a fragile,
    a fossil-like thing half-swallowed
by the unruly bluestem and Indian grass
    bearding the rough face of the prairie.

The way he sat, head cocked,
    studying this long-useless artifact as
closely as one might study one's reflection
    year and year again in alarmed confusion
first suggested dementia, the thieving
    disease that would eventually cause inability
to use a fork, certain words, the toilet,
    but no, this was not that, not yet.

There was still an audible understanding
    in his sigh when you crawled into his lap,
pressing pillowy cheek to sagging cheek,
    enclosing in your fingers his twisted ones
and straining against the obstinacy of time
    to see the same thing he was seeing.

To a Folksinger Just Arrived From the Midwest

Whisper salutations to your irises
and tie those strange ornaments
into your hair. Crawl from your
Volkswagen into the sweltering city
and pluck something evangelical
from your book of songs. Strum
your dulcimer and enunciate as if
to blow life back into fried chicken
or restore the red to petrified roses.
Give them mystery, ancestry.
Give them not too much skin.
Yours, never forget, is the music
of freight trains and holyghosts.
You need only the lungs to drown
out the daily discord, the ambulances,
the ring tones and the burglar alarms,
and the city will place its heart
on the steaming asphalt and ascend.

Last Lesson in Ruin

Of all things holy, barn is holiest.
Barn is crumbling red shaman;
it is old wood and old wood is
porous and good for drinking
up the old man's confessions.

Every scarecrow in tattered
fatigues has his war story
to send up to the gods. Step
forward, scarecrow, and walk
where your knees get lost
in snakegrass and cockleburs.

Ruined things stow away inside
a stout magic of forgiveness.
Find the rusted grain bins. Find
the tractor's bones. Find where
the old women once worked
afternoons behind the clothesline,
faces like influenza, faces carved
from terrible ancient rocks.

Find the house, *find the barn.*
No need to worry—it knows you.
It knows why you have come home.

Rustsong

Rust, you are a Heartland
impressionist painter,

philosophies brailled out
all across your abrasive face.

You, sir, are the very color
of the crater childhood

made in the middle of me,
a coffin suit to keep the corpse

of my Midwest dressed.
But you are mostly beautiful

from afar. In the hard light
of harder times, I expect

you'd've grown less romantic
as you tainted our tools

and sealed our sheds beneath
an imperial crust of yourself, Rust,

and I imagine it would've been
harder to hum this song for you.

Rebekah Just When the Drought Was Ending

But the best thing about Rebekah
was the way she floated always
beneath the scent of woodburn
and dusty Middle America,
her keen ranch-queen convictions
slicing deep and deeper into
the tiniest of daily miseries
with skepticism, demanding always
some proof before she'd concede
this life He pieced together for us
cell by cell with ever shakier Godfingers
contained even one malignancy.

Every bow-legged young bull rider,
every sunburnt farmer of someday
who stopped by to mend a fence
or just to offer genteel salutations
would see her backlit by sunset,
dream her into his own mother
and pray to the essence of the prairie
to do what old bones could not.
And it worked. She survived well enough
to give of herself four more seasons
among luckless kinfolk who every one
drank greedily the blood she squeezed
and felt the cracked lips of dry times less.

As long as there was some great need
into which she could empty herself
she could will the heart to continue
and none of the rules of dying applied,
but she must've seen that the new rain
wasn't baptismal or meant for her restoration.
When those storm clouds finally swelled
and burst into fat miracle drumbeats
she must've felt the change was coming on.
Why else open the windows so wide
with no thought for the evening chill?
Why else cut a hundred wildflowers
and arrange them into fiery clusters
but pour no water into their vases?

The Sting of the Jellyfish

In my daughter's drawings, we resemble
a trio of jellyfish: our pumpkin-
round heads without torsos, our long
inky legs squiggling playfully
down the page before culminating
in feet like oversized breadloaves.
If we are indeed jellyfish, then
we're clearly happy jellyfish, with
our upturned mouths, despite our eyes,
which are empty, oblong, strangely akin
in shape to gourds, potatoes, yellow squash.
These are the figures that cover page
upon page in my writing notebooks,
appear like trademarked logos in
the corners of my wife's grocery lists.
Sometimes they even add a dash
of unintended variety to our
comments on students' papers.
And they are there too, at night,
taped to every surface I pass as I
make my habitual visit to the refrigerator,
a lonely search party of one, intent
upon rescuing the evening's leftovers
from a long life of isolation and mold.
Three happy, healthy jellyfish,
one of us a bit wider and rounder,
a bit topheavy (even for a jellyfish),

but all of us smiling—beaming, really.
And when I look at them, I understand
this is the way my little daughter
believes it will always go for her family.
Sometimes that in itself is enough
so that I return the pork chop to its
cold nest of rice, applesauce, and peas,
re-snap the red Rubbermaid lid
into place, and sneak back to
bed with the burn deep in my belly.
But sometimes nothing is enough,
not even the memory of coming
into the kitchen at first light
way back when I was a seven or eight,
the scrapyard scatterings surrounding
my mother as she lay face down,
asleep again at the table, this a long
time before the heart attacks.
I'd whisper her awake, and she'd
spring up of a sudden, embarrassed,
the butter smeared all the way
from her chin to that small space
between her nose and her upper lip.
Ask her what she was doing and
she would say she didn't know,
and damn if that wasn't the truth of it.
Once the devil turned loose of her
she could remember almost nothing.

The Third Day of Winter

Snow blows across the alfalfa bales,
across the hood of the forgotten Nova.
It spirals through her broken windows.
It piles over her pedals, and it spreads
across her split, foam-showing seats.
        Ditch, fencepost, scattering
of idiot beef cows, loitering, chewing—
black holes die-cut into fabric of field.
Here and there a few inky treeshapes
rising up like dark tentacles, clawing
for a hold on the same scrolling sky.
        And snow again,
in slanting drifts against the barndoor,
tall to the tires of the rust-eaten tractor.

On the other side of this country lane
the cemetery sprawls like a mute city.
From this walking dream it seems I've
arrived above the half-buried headstones.
Here I stop to rest, hand held to my heart.
        Soon enough, I'll need to
find some way to descend the steep hill
down to where my closest kin are kept.
I have these words of reconciliation,
and I'd like to speak them to my mother.
I've been carrying them a long time now,
        and this time I mean to do it.
Nevermind the great white moat between us;
nevermind that the grave is so far down.

God

Construction continues
on the neighbor's new deck.
Throughout the afternoon
my quick glances out the window
are like a time lapse movie.
First, a gaping space where
the old deck used to be.
Next, posts, beams, blocking
and deck boards, fascia and balusters,
as this small thing of beauty
I couldn't build in my dreams
settles into its final shape.
Man over here, man over there.
At the saw, at the cooler, about
to make thunder with his hammer.
What God actually has to do
with any of this is highly uncertain.
I admit I just gave the poem a title
I thought might lend it some gravity.
But now that I am forced to
make some connection or risk
losing you to discouragement,
I'll suppose I'll say that after
all this time I've finally decided—
if He's really up there, He's probably
just a painful introvert, like me,
only with a lot more windows

to glance out of in awe, or terror,
at the endless human documentary,
a lot more reasons to cross Himself
and thank whomever God thanks
He doesn't actually have to buckle on
the tool belt or operate the table saw —
or else who knows what sort of mess
He might make of everything.

A Real Team Effort

And here you'd gone and told yourself
the morning couldn't possibly
get any worse, not after you realized
you'd left your jock strap swinging
from your bedroom doorknob, as you rushed
headlong into the purple prairie morning, late
again for the six am travel bus
and facing the prospect of a doubleheader
behind the dish without proper protection.

And that's when you see it: your mother's
souped-up Camaro comes peeling
into the high school parking lot, skids
to an action-movie stop in front of the bus
just as the driver jerks her into drive,
and now, incredibly, here is your old man
sprinting in desperation, a thief or a madman,
and there is something in his right hand,
something which he has tucked against his side
for protection, as if it were a football
or perhaps an enormous jewel of untold value.

There comes a pounding and the driver
cranks open the side door with impatience,
and then he has your jock, which he has just
received from your panting, sweat-slicked pops,
and he—the driver—is holding it out away

from himself as if it might be radioactive,
and now he's turning, handing it delicately to Coach,
whose face goes cruel with wind sprints
as he turns and passes it off to Klein the freshy,
cursed to the front seats for having ears
too sensitive for upperclassman conversation,
and Klein the freshy hands off to Castillo
the backup catcher who's gunning for your job,
and Castillo with a snicker gives it to Rosenthal,
and Rosenthal—God help him—holds the thing
a second too long and lifts it toward his nose.

Then Martin, Berringer. Then Jonesy and Little Nick.
And so it goes, every man's hands on your jock strap
until it reaches that SOB Looney, two seats up,
Looney who could reach right out and hand it
to you himself, save you that final humiliation,
but instead he passes it to the team manager
who is sitting in the seat directly in front of yours
because she's beautiful and because you planned it that way.
Now she turns and there it is, dangling between you,
frayed and a little off-white from two years of use.
Through the straps you can see her eyes, two dark
lakes where so many other sensitive boys have gone
and gotten themselves thoroughly and finally drowned.

You reach out to take what is yours, and you wonder:
is this what the old broken men think of when they stare
out their windows into empty backyards, swigging
their warm beers and sighing now and then?

Originally from the flatlands of central Illinois, **Justin Hamm** now lives near Twain territory in Missouri. He is the founding editor of *the museum of americana* and the author of three collections of poetry, *The Inheritance, American Ephemeral,* and *Lessons in Ruin,* and a book of photographs entitled *Midwestern*. His poems, stories, photos, and reviews have appeared in *Nimrod, River Styx, The Midwest Quarterly, Sugar House Review, Pittsburgh Poetry Review,* and a host of other publications. Recent work has also been selected for *New Poetry from the Midwest* (New American Press) and the Stanley Hanks Memorial Poetry Prize from the St. Louis Poetry Center. Justin's poetry and photography show, *Midwestern,* has traveled the Midwest region, appearing in a number of galleries over the last two years. In 2019, his poem "Goodbye, Sancho Panza" was studied by approximately 50,000 students worldwide as a part of the World Scholar's Cup curriculum.